Norbert

th

Written and illustrated
by Jonathan Allen

Chapter 1

Erik Madaxe was a very, very bloodthirsty Viking chief. He loved to fight his enemies and steal from their villages.

Erik Madaxe had a son called Norbert. Norbert was not very bloodthirsty at all. He was a very gentle boy.

Erik Madaxe had yellow hair which was long and untidy. He had a yellow beard which had bits of old food in it. He wore a Viking helmet and he carried a sharp sword.

Norbert had red hair which he kept neatly combed. He had a red beard which he kept clean and tidy. He didn't wear a helmet or carry a sword.

Erik Madaxe was very worried about Norbert. Norbert didn't like singing battle songs. He didn't like looking at his father's battle scars. And he didn't like the lessons on stealing and fighting at school. Norbert was not a normal Viking boy.

One day Norbert asked his dad,
"Why can't Vikings be nice to
other people?"
Erik Madaxe was very angry.
"Nice?" he yelled. "Nice? Vikings
aren't nice. I didn't get where
I am today by being nice.
You don't get called 'Bloodbath
Madaxe' by being nice to people."

The day came when Norbert was eighteen. When the son of a Viking chief is eighteen, he is given his first longship. It is the most important day of his life.

So on Norbert's eighteenth birthday, Erik Madaxe gave him his first Viking longship. It could carry twenty fighting men. It had twenty Viking shields and it could carry lots of swords and axes. But the best thing about it was the fierce dragon head at the front.

“Here you are,” said Erik Madaxe.
“Now you are captain of this ship
you will become a real Viking.
You can attack other ships and
steal from other villages.
You can fight all day long.
In time you will be known as
‘Norbert the Nasty’.”

Norbert thanked his dad and
climbed on board his ship.
Erik Madaxe wiped a tear from his
eye as Norbert and his men set sail.
"We'll make a fighting Viking out of
you after all," he said.

But as soon as the longship had sailed round the corner, Norbert ordered his men to row to a nearby island.
There he unpacked a box that he had hidden on the longship the night before.

Inside the box was a new sail which had a smiley face painted on it. There were new shields, too, with smiley faces on. Norbert ordered his men to put up the new sail and to put the new shields over the ship's sides.

Then Norbert gave the men some pink ribbons to tie up their hair and beards. And he gave them all nice woolly hats to wear instead of their helmets. "We don't want anyone to get cold now do we?" said Norbert.

Then Norbert showed the men what he wanted to put in place of the fierce dragon head. It was a pink fluffy bunny!

"We will show the world what nice people Vikings are," said Norbert, proudly.

The men did not like Norbert's plans. They hated wearing the pink ribbons and the woolly hats.

And they hated the pink fluffy bunny on the front of the longship.

Next Norbert set about teaching
the men to be polite.
They had to smile and say things like:
“My name is Thor Manslayer.
How may I help you?”
The men were not very happy.

Norbert told the men that there would be no swearing on the longship.
If they felt very angry they were to say things like: "Oh deary me!" or
"Oh bother!"
The men were not happy at all.

When Norbert was happy that his longship looked right, and his men were neat and tidy and always polite, he gave the order to set sail.

Chapter 2

The longship sailed to the next island. On the island was a boy whose job it was to look out for Viking longships. He was bored with his job as there hadn't been any Viking longships for ages. He was just about to fall asleep when he saw a square sail in the distance.

"Vikings! Vikings!" the boy shouted as loudly as he could. "Run and hide! The Vikings are coming!"

The villagers grabbed what they could and ran off to hide in the hills. They knew that when the Vikings came they would steal anything they found. And fight anyone they saw.

Norbert and his men landed on
the shore of the island.
At once his men grabbed their
swords and axes and began to
wave them about.
"No, no!" said Norbert. "What are
you doing? Have you forgotten
everything I told you? We come here
in peace."

"In peace?" said one of the men.
"What's that?"
"Oh dear!" said Norbert. "You have so much to learn."
Norbert took away each man's sword and axe and gave them a dustpan and brush or a mop and bucket.
"Now, follow me!" he shouted.
And feeling rather silly, the men followed Norbert into the village.

The village was empty because
everyone was hiding from the Vikings.
Norbert gave orders that each
house was to be swept clean and
each floor was to be mopped.
The men worked for hours, sweeping
and mopping.
"This is harder work than stealing
and fighting," said one man.

Then Norbert went into every house in the village to check that it was clean. He looked in the corners for dust and he looked under the beds for dirt. If he found any dust or dirt, he would say to the men, "Oh deary me! You must clean this house again."

At last every house in the village was clean. Norbert was very pleased. He went into the last house and put a vase of flowers on the table. Next to the vase he put a note which said:

Norbert and his men went
back to their longship.
The men were very fed up.
"No stealing," said one man, sadly.
"No fighting," said another man.
"Oh deary me!" they all said.

When the Vikings had gone, the villagers began to return to their houses. At first they couldn't believe their eyes. Nothing had been burnt. Nothing had been stolen. And nobody had been attacked. It was very odd.

Norbert and his men sailed
on to other islands.
In each village they swept and mopped,
they polished and dusted and they
left flowers on the tables.
The men were not happy but they
were afraid. If they disobeyed Norbert,
then his father, Erik Madaxe, might
come after them.

So they did what Norbert told them.

"Life is no fun anymore," said one man.

"I miss the stealing," said another man.

"And the fighting," said a third man.

"Oh deary me!" they all said.

Norbert saw how unhappy his men were. He wanted to cheer them up. "I know," he said, "let's go back to that first village. The people will be really pleased to see us.
They will want to thank us.
They may even hold a feast for us."

Chapter 3

Norbert and his men set
sail back to the first island.
They landed on the shore and
slowly walked up to the village.
But to their surprise the village was
empty. Everyone had run to the
hills to hide from the Vikings.

Norbert went into the first house.
He let out a great cry.
His men came running in.
"What's the matter?" they asked.
"Look! Look!" cried Norbert.
The men looked. The house was a mess.

There was dust everywhere and
the floor was filthy.
Norbert was very angry.
Even the men felt a bit sad.
All that hard work and nothing to
show for it!

Norbert and his men ran from house to house. It was the same in each house. Dust everywhere. Filthy floors. What a mess!

Norbert ran into the last house.
"Oh no! Oh no!" he cried.
The men ran in after him.
They saw the vase that Norbert had left full of flowers. It was in a corner.
The villagers had been using it – but not for flowers!
"Phew!" said the Vikings.

Some of the villagers had come
back down to the village.
They had seen the smiley face on the sail
and knew it was the *softy* Vikings.
They began to tease Norbert and
his men.
They called out, "Hey! Vikings!
Clear off or we'll pull your pink ribbons!"

Norbert went out into the street.
"Now look here," he said.
"We came in peace to show you
how nice Vikings really are.
We dusted your houses and
we mopped your floors.
Now you've let them get all dirty
again. And as for my vase ..."

Norbert did not finish what he was saying because a stone came flying through the air and hit him on the head.

"Clear off you softy Vikings!" called the villagers.

Norbert's face turned pink.

Then it went red.

Then purple.

He opened his mouth and let out a roar that made the houses shake. "That's how you thank us is it?" he shouted. "Well, no more Mr Nice Viking. Come on lads. Get stuck in!"

Norbert charged at the nearest villager, using his mop as a spear. When his men saw Norbert fighting, they tore off their pink ribbons and joined in!

The villagers didn't stand a chance.
Norbert and his men attacked
using dustpans and mops.
It was not a pretty sight.

Norbert and his men set fire to the village and ran back to their longship. Only two people in the village lived to tell the saga of 'The Battle of the Dustpans and Mops'.

"Well, I can't say it was much fun," said the first man, "but at least they did what you expect Vikings to do."

"Yes," said the other man, "steal and fight!"

Norbert and his men went back to the island where they had left their Viking sail and shields.

"No more smiley faces on the shields," said Norbert. "And I need to make a few changes to the sail."

Then Norbert took off the pink fluffy rabbit head and put back the dragon head. All the men gave a loud cheer.

Hooray!
Hooray!

Next the men made a big fire.
Into the fire they threw the
dustpans and the brushes,
the mops and the buckets,
and the smiley face shields.
And on top of the fire, Norbert
put the pink fluffy rabbit!

Then Norbert and his men sailed across the seas. When they came to a village, they would steal and fight. And nobody did more stealing and fighting than Norbert.

And in time he came to be known as 'Norbert the Nasty'.

When Erik Madaxe heard about Norbert, he said proudly, "That's my boy!"